A Thought fo

A Year's Journey into Awareness

With Irish Mindfulness

By Julie Ruane

January 1

New dawn, new beginning, a new chapter in your life beckons.

January 2

Let us look forward with hope, and look around with love.

January 3

Do not cloud the present moment, with the regrets of the past and the fears of tomorrow.

January 4

Money can buy a better standard of living, but not happiness.

January 5

"Ní hé lá na gaoithe lá na scoilb". A windy day is not a day for thatching.

January 6

Never judge another, until you have walked in their shoes.

January 7

"I scath a chéile a mhaireann na daoine" - In each other's shadow the people live.

January 8

Friends are the family we chose for ourselves.

January 9

Never listen to those who say it can't be done, forge a new path.

January 10

Be a lighthouse for those around you.

January 11

Invest time, energy and love in your children. They hold the key to the future.

January 12

Every disappointment offers a lesson for learning.

January 13

"The essence of bravery is being without self-deception." Pema Chödrön

January 14

The sunshine of your smile can chase away the clouds for another.

January 15

"Be there a will, and wisdom finds a way." George Crabbe

January 16

Whenever you can replace a vice with a virtue.

January 17

"Begin, be bold and venture to be wise." Horace

January 18

"Nothing ever goes away until it has taught us what we need to know." Pema Chödrön   *What you resist, persists.*

January 19

Live your own life. Have no regrets.

January 20

Life is not a dress rehearsal

January 21

Love is the key   *Love is all there is.*

January 22

"Altogether, the idea of meditation is not to create states of ecstasy or absorption, but to experience being." Chögyam Trungpa

January 23

"That's life: starting over, one breath at a time." Sharon Salzberg

January 25

"Ní mar a shíltear a bhítear". What is assumed is often wrong.

January 26

The winds of change sweep over all of us.

January 27

"What would it be like if I could accept life – accept this moment – exactly as it is?" Tara Brach

January 28

Time waits for no one.

January 29

"Wisdom consists not so much in knowing what to do in the ultimate as knowing what to do next." Herbert Hoover

January 30

"The more tranquil a man becomes, the greater is his success, his influence, his power for good." James Allen

January 31

"If you have the guts to keep making mistakes, your wisdom and intelligence leap forward with huge momentum." Holly Near

February 1

"Is maith an t-anlann an t-ocras." Before a big meal after a long fast. ~~X~~ *Enjoy*

Hunger is the best sauce.

February 2

"Be yourself, everyone else is taken"- Oscar Wilde

February 3

"Mindfulness means being awake. It means knowing what you are doing." Jon Kabat-Zinn

February 4

"Begin at once to live, and count each separate day as a separate life." Seneca

February 5

"Today, like every other day, we wake up empty and frightened. Don't open the door to the study and begin reading. Take down a musical instrument." Rumi

February 6

"Blessed is the man who, having nothing to say, abstains from giving wordy evidence of the fact". George Eliot

February 7

"Adopt the pace of nature: her secret is patience." Ralph Waldo Emerson

February 8

"The softest things in the world overcome the hardest things in the world." Lao Tzu

February 9

"Giorraíonn beirt bother." A companion shortens a road.

February 10

 "Observe the space between your thoughts, then observe the observer." Hamilton Boudreaux

February 11

"In every walk with nature one receives far more than he seeks." John Muir

February 12

"Is minic a bhris béal duine a shrón." It is often a man's mouth broke his nose.

February 13

"We don't receive wisdom; we must discover it for ourselves after a journey that no one can take for us or spare us." Marcel Proust

February 14

"All you need is love". The Beatles

February 15

"Happiness is a journey, not a destination". Souza

February 16

"Life is not lost by dying; life is lost minute by minute, day by dragging day, in all the small uncaring ways." Stephen Vincent Benet

February 17

"If you want to conquer the anxiety of life, live in the moment, live in the breath." Amit Ray

February 18

"A man has made at least a start on discovering the meaning of human life when he plants shade trees under which he knows full well he will never sit." David Elton Trueblood

February 19

"The motto of chivalry is also the motto of wisdom; to serve all, but love only one". Honore De Balzac

February 20

"Ni beireann cailin dathuil an citeal." Beauty doesn't boil the kettle.

February 21

"Work like you don't need the money. Love like you've never been hurt. Dance like nobody's watching." Satchel Paige

February 22

"If the doors of perception were cleansed, everything would appear to man as it is, infinite." William Blake

February 23

"Knowing others is wisdom, knowing yourself is Enlightenment." Lao Tzu

February 24

"Feelings come and go like clouds in a windy sky. Conscious breathing is my anchor." Thich Nhat Hanh

February 25

"He gossips habitually; he lacks the common wisdom to keep still that deadly enemy of man, his own tongue." Mark Twain

February 26

Say "yes" to life and all it's facets

February 27

"Is olc an ghaoth nach séideann do dhuine éigin." It is a bad wind that does not bring good to someone.

February 28

"Who then is free? The wise man who can command himself." Horace

March 1

"Everything comes in time to him who knows how to wait." Leo Tolst

March 2

"If you want to conquer the anxiety of life, live in the moment, live in the breath." Amit Ray

March 3

"In the end, just three things matter: How well we have lived. How well we have loved. How well we have learned to let go" Jack Kornfield

March 4

"Do every act of your life as though it were the last act of your life." Marcus Aurelius

March 5

"Everything is created twice, first in the mind and then in reality." Robin S. Sharma

March 6

Open the window of your mind, and allow new thoughts to enter.

March 7

"An sean madra don bhóthar chruaidh." The old dog for the hard road.

March 8

Your mind can access infinite intelligence.

March 9

"Much of spiritual life is self-acceptance, maybe all of it." Jack Kornfield

March 10

"You are the sky. Everything else is just the weather." Pema Chödrön

March 11

"No one has ever been angry at another human being we're only angry at our story of them." Byron Katie

March 12

"An té a luíonn le madaí, eireoidh sé le dearnaid." He who lies down with the dogs, gets up with fleas.

March 13

"A few simple tips for life: feet on the ground, head to the skies, heart open…quiet mind." Rasheed Ogunlaru

March 14

We have two ears and one mouth for a reason. Let us listen to each other.

March 15

Every new day is a gift of possibility and potential.

March 16

Relax, be still and tune in to the inner voice of wisdom.

March 17

I'm Irish. What's your super-power?

March 18

Every moment is part of eternity.

March 19

Saying "no" is the supreme self-care. Mind yourself.

March 20

Look again with the eyes of a child.

March 21

"Be there a will, and wisdom finds a way. " George Crabbe

March 22

"Níl saoi gan locht." There's not a wise man without fault

March 23

Take a moment to be still in the midst of the daily busy-ness

March 24

Nobody is perfect. But you are unique.

March 25

Acceptance of self, is the beginning of growth.

March 26

"He who would begun has half done. Dare to be wise; begin." Horace

March 27

"He that composes himself is wiser than he that composes a book". B. Franklin.

March 28

"Filleann an feall ar an bhfeallaire." The bad deed returns to the perpetrator

March 29

"Stronger by weakness, wiser men become". Edmund Waller

March 30

"Begin, be bold and venture to be wise." Horace

March 31

Love is the key.

April 1

Smile- it's contagious!

April 2

"The best way to capture moments is to pay attention. This is how we cultivate mindfulness." Jon Kabat-Zinn

April 3

"Don't let life harden your heart." Pema Chödrön

April 4

Inhale and exhale, and go with the flow

April 5

You can never step into the same river twice.

April 6

"Mindfulness means being awake. It means knowing what you are doing." Jon Kabat-Zinn

April 7

"The little things? The little moments? They aren't little." Jon Kabat-Zinn

April 8

Life is as simple as you make it.

April 9

"Mindfulness is a way of befriending ourselves and our experience." Jon Kabat-Zinn

April 10

Perform one random act of Kindness regularly.

April 11

"How you look at it is pretty much how you'll see it." Rasheed Ogunlaru

April 12

Be here, right now, and savour the moment

April 13

"The Way is not in the sky, the Way is in the heart." Buddha

April 14

Take 5 long deep breaths when you start the day

April 15

Be your own best friend.

April 16

"You only lose what you cling to." Buddha

April 17

"In today's rush, we all think too much — seek too much — want too much — and forget about the joy of just being." Eckhart Tolle

April 18

"Wanting to reform the world without discovering one's true self is like trying to cover the world with leather to avoid the pain of walking on stones and thorns. It is much simpler to wear shoes." Ramana Maharshi

April 19

 "Looking at beauty in the world, is the first step of purifying the mind." Amit Ray

April 20

All the answers you seek are within. Listen carefully.

April 21

"In this moment, there is plenty of time. In this moment, you are precisely as you should be. In this moment, there is infinite possibility." Victoria Moran

April 22

"Training your mind to be in the present moment is the #1 key to making healthier choices." Susan Albers

April 23

"The best way to capture moments is to pay attention. This is how we cultivate mindfulness." Jon Kabat-Zinn

April 24

"Observe the space between your thoughts, then observe the observer."
Hamilton Boudreaux

April 25

"One who is patient glows with an inner radiance." Allan Lokos

April 26

"Being mindful means that we suspend judgment for a time, set aside our immediate goals for the future, and take in the present moment as it is rather than as we would like it to be." Mark Williams.

April 27

"Until you realize how easily it is for your mind to be manipulated, you remain the puppet of someone else's game." Evita Ochel

April 28

"Knowledge does not mean mastering a great quantity of different information, but understanding the nature of mind. This knowledge can penetrate each one of our thoughts and illuminate each one of our perceptions." Matthieu Ricard

April 29

"Don't believe everything you think. Thoughts are just that – thoughts." Allan Lokos

April 30

"Everything is created twice, first in the mind and then in reality." Robin S. Sharma

April 31

Practice 5 deep breaths daily.

May 1

"It's only when we truly know and understand that we have a limited time on earth – that we will begin to live each day to the fullest, as if it was the only one we had." Elisabeth Kübler-Ross

May 2

"Today, like every other day, we wake up empty and frightened. Don't open the door to the study and begin reading. Take down a musical instrument." Rumi

May 3

Mindfulness means being awake. It means knowing what you are doing." Jon Kabat-Zinn

May 4

"When I'm bored, I do something I love. When I'm lonely, I connect with someone I love. When I feel sad, I remember that I am loved." – Michelle May

May 5

Remember you are a unique child of the universe.

May 6

"You can't stop the waves, but you can learn to surf." Jon Kabat-Zinn

May 7

"Nothing is forever except change." Buddha

May 8

"The stiller you are the calmer life is." Rasheed Ogunlaru

May 9

Go inside and listen to your inner wisdom.

May 10

"Three things cannot hide for long: the Moon, the Sun and the Truth." Buddha

May 11

"Every problem perceived to be 'out there' is really nothing more than a misperception within your own thinking." Byron Katie

May 12

"Few of us ever live in the present. We are forever anticipating what is to come or remembering what has gone." Louis L'Amour

May 13

"Step outside for a while – calm your mind. It is better to hug a tree than to bang your head against a wall continually." Rasheed Ogunlaru

May 14

"You must be completely awake in the present to enjoy it." Thích Nhất Hạnh

May 15

Always aim to maintain a work-life balance

May 16

Life is for living- enjoy!

May 17

"Looking at beauty in the world, is the first step of purifying the mind." Amit Ray

May 18

"Ní dhéanfadh an saol capall rása d'asal." You can't make a racehorse out of a donkey

May 19

If you want to conquer the anxiety of life, aim to live in the moment.

May 20

"Peace comes from within. Do not seek it without." Buddha

May 21

"Your actions are your only true belongings." Allan Lokos

May 22

"Mindfulness isn't difficult, we just need to remember to do it." Sharon Salzberg

May 23

"If the problem can be solved why worry? If the problem cannot be solved worrying will do you no good." Buddha

May 24

Rejoice in ordinary things.

May 25

"Every time we become aware of a thought, as opposed to being lost in a thought, we experience that opening of the mind." Joseph Goldstein

May 26

"Use every distraction as an object of meditation and they cease to be distractions." Mingyur Rinpoche

May 27

"The mind is just like a muscle – the more you exercise it, the stronger it gets and the more it can expand." Idowu Koyenikan

<u>May 28</u>

Concentration is a cornerstone of mindfulness practice.

<u>May 29</u>

"Dá fhada an lá tagann an tráthnóna." No matter how long the day is, the evening always comes.

<u>May 30</u>

"Why, if we are as pragmatic as we claim, don't we begin to ask ourselves seriously: Where does our real future lie?" Sogyal Rinpoche

<u>May 31</u>

Enjoy the warmth of the sun's rays on your face.

June 1

"If you concentrate on finding whatever is good in every situation, you will discover that your life will suddenly be filled with gratitude, a feeling that nurtures the soul." ~Rabbi Harold Kushner

June 2

"There's only one reason why you're not experiencing bliss at this present moment, and it's because you're thinking or focusing on what you don't have…. But, right now you have everything you need to be in bliss." Anthony de Mello

June 3

"Our own worst enemy cannot harm us as much as our unwise thoughts. No one can help us as much as our own compassionate thoughts." Buddha

June 4

"Observe the space between your thoughts, then observe the observer." Hamilton Boudreaux.

June 5

"The practice of mindfulness begins in the small, remote cave of your unconscious mind and blossoms with the sunlight of your conscious life, reaching far beyond the people and places you can see." Earon Davis

June 6

"Life is not lost by dying; life is lost minute by minute, day by dragging day, in all the small uncaring ways." Stephen Vincent Benet

June 7

"The mind is just like a muscle – the more you exercise it, the stronger it gets and the more it can expand." Idowu Koyenikan

June 8

"As long as we have practiced neither concentration nor mindfulness, the ego takes itself for granted and remains its usual normal size, as big as the people around one will allow." Ayya Khema

June 9

change

"Impermanence is a principle of harmony. When we don't struggle against it, we are in harmony with reality." Pema Chodron

June 10

"The basic root of happiness lies in our minds; outer circumstances are nothing more than adverse or favourable." Matthieu Ricard

June 11

"The mind in its natural state can be compared to the sky, covered by layers of cloud which hide its true nature." Kalu Rinpoche

June 12

"Be kind whenever possible. It is always possible." Dalai Lama

June 13

"If one were truly aware of the value of human life, to waste it blithely on distractions and the pursuit of vulgar ambitions would be the height of confusion." Dilgo Khyentse Rinpoche

June 14

"Knowledge does not mean mastering a great quantity of different information, but understanding the nature of mind. This knowledge can penetrate each one of our thoughts and illuminate each one of our perceptions." Matthieu Ricard

June 15

"Ní neart go cur le chéile." There is strength in unity.

June 16

"The most precious gift we can offer others is our presence. When mindfulness embraces those we love, they will bloom like flowers." Thich Nhat Hanh

June 17

"We are awakened to the profound realization that the true path to liberation is to let go of everything." Jack Kornfield

June 18

"To diminish the suffering of pain, we need to make a crucial distinction between the pain of pain, and the pain we create by our thoughts about the pain." Howard Cutler

June 19

"Things falling apart is a kind of testing and also a kind of healing." Pema Chodron

June 20

"Envy and jealousy stem from the fundamental inability to rejoice at someone else's happiness or success." Matthieu Ricard

June 21

"Essentially, meditation allows us to live in ways that are less automatic. It means we become less vulnerable to the throes of the fear-driven parts of our brains, and freer to use our newer mental abilities: patience, compassion, acceptance and reason." David Cain

June 22

By breaking down our sense of self-importance, we gain freedom, openness of mind, spontaneity and happiness.

June 23

"An rud is annamh is iontach." What is seldom is wonderful

June 24

"Our lives are lived in intense and anxious struggle, in a swirl of speed and aggression, in competing, grasping, possessing and achieving, forever burdening ourselves with extraneous activities and preoccupations." Sogyal Rinpoche

June 25

"We have only now, only this single eternal moment opening and unfolding before us, day and night." Jack Kornfield

June 26

"Mindful and creative, a child who has neither a past, nor examples to follow, nor value judgments, simply lives, speaks and plays in freedom." Arnaud Desjardins

June 27

"Feelings come and go like clouds in a windy sky. Conscious breathing is my anchor." Thich Nhat Hanh

June 28

"Is ait an mac an saol." Life is strange

June 29

"Concentrate the mind on the present moment." Buddha

June 30

"Do every act of your life as though it were the very last act of your life." Marcus Aurelius

July 1

Life is a dance, enjoy the music

July 2

"It is never too late to turn on the light." Sharon Salzberg

July 3

"You can't stop the waves, but you can learn to surf." Jon Kabat-Zinn

July 4

"Treat everyone you meet as if they were you." Doug Dillon

July 5

"Every morning we are born again. What we do today is what matters most."
 Buddha

July 6

"A mind set in its ways is wasted." Eric Schmidt

July 7

"Do not dwell in the past, do not dream of the future, concentrate the mind on the present moment." Buddha

July 8

"We are awakened to the profound realization that the true path to liberation is to let go of everything." Jack Kornfield

July 9

"Begin at once to live, and count each separate day as a separate life." Seneca

July 10

Fear, anger, guilt, loneliness and helplessness are all mental and emotional responses to our thought patterns.

July 11

Begin to ask yourself seriously- where does your real future lie?

July 12

"Things falling apart is a kind of testing and also a kind of healing." Pema Chodron

July 13

Envy and jealousy stem from the fundamental inability to rejoice at someone else's happiness. Let us change our ways.

July 14

"Today, like every other day, we wake up empty and frightened. Don't open the door to the study and begin reading. Take down a musical instrument." Rumi

July 15

"I wish that life should not be cheap, but sacred. I wish the days to be as centuries, loaded, fragrant." Ralph Waldo Emerson

July 16

Each morning we can start again. What we do today is what matters.

July 17

The present is a gift to you, for you.

July 18

"Always hold fast to the present. Every situation, indeed every moment, is of infinite value, for it is the representative of a whole eternity." Johann Wolfgang von Goethe

July 19

"Níl aon tinteán mar do thinteán féin." There is no place like home.

July 20

"If you concentrate on finding whatever is good in every situation, you will discover that your life will suddenly be filled with gratitude, a feeling that nurtures the soul." Rabbi Harold Kushner

July 21

Our own negative thoughts can cause so much harm. Be careful what you think about.

July 22

"There's only one reason why you're not experiencing bliss at this present moment, and it's because you're thinking or focusing on what you don't have.... But, right now you have everything you need to be in bliss." Anthony de Mello

July 23

"Observe the space between your thoughts, then observe the observer." Hamilton Boudreaux

July 24

"Our own worst enemy cannot harm us as much as our unwise thoughts. No one can help us as much as our own compassionate thoughts." Buddha

July 25

"Things falling apart is a kind of testing and also a kind of healing." Pema Chodron

July 26

"In today's rush, we all think too much — seek too much — want too much — and forget about the joy of just being." Eckhart Tolle

July 27

"Wanting to reform the world without discovering one's true self is like trying to cover the world with leather to avoid the pain of walking on stones and thorns. It is much simpler to wear shoes. Ramana Maharshi

July 28

"Looking at beauty in the world, is the first step of purifying the mind." Amit Ray

July 29

"In this moment, there is plenty of time. In this moment, you are precisely as you should be. In this moment, there is infinite possibility." Victoria Moran

July 30

"Inis do Mháire i gcógar é, is inseoidh Máire do phóbal é." Tell Mary a secret and she will tell everyone.

July 31

"Training your mind to be in the present moment is the #1 key to making healthier choices." Susan Albers

<u>August 1</u>

"The best way to capture moments is to pay attention. This is how we cultivate mindfulness." Jon Kabat-Zinn

<u>August 2</u>

"Observe the space between your thoughts, then observe the observer." Hamilton Boudreaux

<u>August 3</u>

"One who is patient glows with an inner radiance." Allan Lokos

<u>August 4</u>

"Being mindful means that we suspend judgment for a time, set aside our immediate goals for the future, and take in the present moment as it is." Mark Williams

<u>August 5</u>

"Until you realize how easily it is for your mind to be manipulated, you remain the puppet of someone else's game." Evita Ochel

August 6

"Knowledge does not mean mastering a great quantity of different information, but understanding the nature of mind. This knowledge can penetrate each one of our thoughts and illuminate each one of our perceptions." Matthieu Ricard

August 7

"You can't stop the waves, but you can learn to surf." Jon Kabat-Zinn

August 8

"Everything is created twice, first in the mind and then in reality." Robin S. Sharma

August 9

"It's only when we understand that we have a limited time, we will begin to live each day to the fullest." Elisabeth Kübler-Ross

August 10

"Don't believe everything you think. Thoughts are just that – thoughts." Allan Lokos

August 11

Mindfulness means being awake. It means knowing what you are doing." Jon Kabat-Zinn

August 12

"Today, like every other day, we wake up empty and frightened. Don't open the door to the study and begin reading. Take down a musical instrument."   Rumi

August 13

"Wherever you are, be there totally." Eckhart Tolle

August 14

"If you concentrate on finding whatever is good in every situation, you will discover that your life will suddenly be filled with gratitude, a feeling that nurtures the soul." Rabbi Harold Kushner

August 15

"If you clean the floor with love, you have given the world an invisible painting." Osho

August 16

"Mindfulness means being awake. It means knowing what you are doing." Jon Kabat-Zinn

August 17

"Do not ruin today with mourning tomorrow." Catherynne M. Valente

August 18

"Everything that has a beginning has an ending. Make your peace with that and all will be well." Jack Kornfield

August 19

"Flow with whatever may happen and let your mind be free: Stay centred by accepting whatever you are doing. This is the ultimate." Chuang

August 20

"Life is better when we don't try to do everything. Learn to enjoy the slice of life you experience, and life turns out to be wonderful." Leo Babauta

August 21

A choppy surface and will not be able to reflect things with any accuracy.

August 22

"Life is a dance. Mindfulness is witnessing that dance." Amit Ray

August 23

"We might begin by scanning our body . . . and then asking, "What is happening?" We might also ask, "What wants my attention right now?" or "What is asking for acceptance?" Tara Brach

August 24

"Altogether, the idea of meditation is not to create states of ecstasy or absorption, but to experience being." Chögyam Trungpa

August 25

"Meditate … do not delay, lest you later regret it." Buddha

August 26

"I believe in not trying to control things that are out of my control or none of my business." Tobe Hanson

August 27

"The basic root of happiness lies in our minds; outer circumstances are nothing more than adverse or favourable." Matthieu Ricard

August 28

"Wherever you are, be there totally." Eckhart Tolle

August 29

"If you concentrate on finding whatever is good in every situation, you will discover that your life will suddenly be filled with gratitude, a feeling that nurtures the soul." Rabbi Harold Kushner

August 30

"An té nach bhfuil láidir, ní foláir dó bheith glic." He who is not strong, must be clever

August 31

There is no place like home.

September 1

"If you clean the floor with love, you have given the world an invisible painting." Osho

September 2

"Mindfulness means being awake. It means knowing what you are doing." Jon Kabat-Zinn

September 3

"Do not ruin today with mourning tomorrow." Catherynne M. Valente

September 4

"Everything that has a beginning has an ending. Make your peace with that and all will be well." Jack Kornfield

September 5

 Learn to enjoy the slice of life you experience.

September 6

"Flow with whatever may happen and let your mind be free: Stay centred by accepting whatever you are doing. This is the ultimate." Chuang

September 7

"Training your mind to be in the present moment is the #1 key to making healthier choices." Susan Albers

September 8

"The best way to capture moments is to pay attention. " Jon Kabat-Zinn

September 9

"Observe the space between your thoughts, then observe the observer." Hamilton Boudreaux

September 10

"One who is patient glows with an inner radiance." Allan Lokos

September 11

"Being mindful means that we take in the present moment as it is rather than as we would like it to be." Mark Williams

September 12

"Knowledge does not mean mastering a great quantity of different information, but understanding the nature of mind." Matthieu Ricard

September 13

"Until you realize how easily it is for your mind to be manipulated, you remain the puppet of someone else's game." Evita Ochel

September 14

Thoughts are just that – thoughts.

September 15

"Is treise an dúchas ná an oiliúint." Nature is stronger than nurture.

September 16

"When you bow, you should just bow; when you sit, you should just sit; when you eat, you should just eat." Shunryu Suzuki

September 17

"Tea is an act complete in its simplicity. When I drink tea, there is only me and the tea. The rest of the world dissolves." Thích Nhất Hạnh

September 18

"Observe the space between your thoughts, then observe the observer." Hamilton Boudreaux

September 19

"The practice of mindfulness begins in the small, remote cave of your unconscious mind and blossoms with the sunlight of your conscious life, reaching far beyond the people and places you can see." Earon Davis

September 20

"Life is not lost by dying; life is lost minute by minute, day by dragging day, in all the small uncaring ways." Stephen Vincent Benet

September 21

"As long as we have practiced neither concentration nor mindfulness, the ego takes itself for granted and remains its usual normal size, as big as the people around one will allow." Ayya Khema

September 22

"Impermanence is a principle of harmony. When we don't struggle against it, we are in harmony with reality." Pema Chodron

September 23

"The basic root of happiness lies in our minds; outer circumstances are nothing more than adverse or favourable." Matthieu Ricard

September 24

"The mind in its natural state can be compared to the sky, covered by layers of cloud which hide its true nature." Kalu Rinpoche

September 25

"Be kind whenever possible. It is always possible." Dalai Lama

September 26

"Each step along the Buddha's path to happiness requires practising mindfulness until it becomes part of your daily life." Henepola Gunaratana

September 27

"Mol an óige agus tiocfaidh sí." Praise youth and they will respond.

<u>September 28</u>

"Mindfulness isn't difficult, we just need to remember to do it." Sharon Salzberg

<u>September 29</u>

"Walk as if you are kissing the Earth with your feet." Thich Nhat Hanh

<u>September 30</u>

"Every time we become aware of a thought, as opposed to being lost in a thought, we experience that opening of the mind." Joseph Goldstein

October 1

"Concentration is a cornerstone of mindfulness practice. Your mindfulness will only be as robust as the capacity of your mind to be calm and stable." Jon Kabat-Zinn

October 2

"Feelings come and go like clouds in a windy sky. Conscious breathing is my anchor." Thich Nhat Hanh

October 3

"The greatest communication is usually how we are rather than what we say." Joseph Goldstein

October 4

"Meditation is essentially training our attention so that we can be more aware— not only of our own inner workings but also of what's happening around us in the here & now." Sharon Salzberg

October 5

"Wherever you are, be there totally." Eckhart Tolle

October 6

Saturate every atom. Give the moment whole; whatever it requires.

October 7

"The best way to capture moments is to pay attention. This is how we cultivate mindfulness. Mindfulness means being awake. It means knowing what you are doing." Jon Kabat-Zinn

October 8

"What you are looking for is what is looking." Joseph Goldstein

October 9

"Do every act of your life as though it were the last act of your life." Marcus Aurelius

October 10

"If you miss the present moment, you miss your appointment with life. That is very serious!" Thich Nhat Hanh

October 11

"Meditate … do not delay, lest you later regret it." The Buddha

October 12

"Mindful and creative, a child who has neither a past, nor examples to follow, nor value judgments, simply lives, speaks and plays in freedom." Arnaud Desjardins

October 13

"Ní heolas go haontíos." You must live with a person to know a person.

October 14

"Flow with whatever may happen and let your mind be free: Stay centred by accepting whatever you are doing. This is the ultimate." Chuang

October 15

"When you do something, you should burn yourself up completely, like a good bonfire, leaving no trace of yourself." Shunryu Suzuki

October 16

"Practice is this life, and realization is this life, and this life is revealed right here and now." Maezumi Roshi

October 17

"Emotion arises at the place where mind & body meet. It is the body's reaction to mind." Eckhart Tolle

October 18

"Use every distraction as an object of meditation and they cease to be distractions." Mingyur Rinpoche

October 19

"Is minic a rinne bromach gioblach capall". A raggy colt often made a powerful horse.

October 20

"Feelings come and go like clouds in a windy sky. Conscious breathing is my anchor." Thich Nhat Hanh

October 21

"The greatest communication is usually how we are rather than what we say." Joseph Goldstein

October 22

"Meditation is essentially training our attention so that we can be more aware- in the here & now." Sharon Salzberg

October 23

"Wherever you are, be there totally." Eckhart Tolle

October 24

"Mindfulness means being awake. It means knowing what you are doing." Jon Kabat-Zinn

October 25

"What you are looking for is what is looking." Joseph Goldstein

October 26

"Do every act of your life as though it were the last act of your life." Marcus Aurelius

October 27

"If you miss the present moment, you miss your appointment with life. That is very serious!" Thich Nhat Hanh

October 28

"Be something to someone." Dermot Kennedy

October 29

 "Mindful and creative, a child who has neither a past, nor examples to follow, nor value judgments, simply lives, speaks and plays in freedom." Arnaud Desjardins

October 30

"Tá onóir ag an aois agus uaisle ag an óige." Age is honourable and youth is noble

October 31

 "When you do something, you should burn yourself up completely, like a good bonfire, leaving no trace of yourself." Shunryu Suzuki

November 1

"Practice is this life, and realization is this life, and this life is revealed right here and now." Maezumi Roshi

November 2

It is the body's reaction to mind." Eckhart Tolle

November 3

"Use every distraction as an object of meditation and they cease to be distractions." Mingyur Rinpoche

November 4

"Now is the future that you promised yourself . Mindfulness is about waking up to this." Mark Williams

November 5

"Ní mhaireann rith maith ag an each i gcónaí." The steed does not keep his speed forever.

November 6

"Happiness is your nature. It is not wrong to desire it. What is wrong is seeking it outside when it is inside." Ramana Maharshi

November 7

"Ardently do today what must be done. Who knows? Tomorrow, death comes."
Buddha

November 8

"Wanting to reform the world without discovering one's true self is like trying
to cover the world with leather to avoid the pain of walking on stones." Ramana
Maharshi

November 9

"People usually consider walking on water or in thin air a miracle. But I think
the real miracle is not to walk either on water or in thin air, but to walk on earth.
Thích Nhat Hanh

November 10

"Your vision will become clear only when you look into your heart. Who looks
outside, dreams. Who looks inside, awakens." Carl Jung

November 11

"As I noticed feelings and thoughts appear and disappear, it became
increasingly clear that they were just coming and going on their own." Tara
Brach

November 12

"Meditation is the only intentional, systematic human activity which at bottom is about not trying to improve yourself or get anywhere else, but simply to realize where you already are." Jon Kabat-Zinn

November 13

"Awareness is the greatest agent for change." Eckhart Tolle

November 14

"Reality is only an agreement - today is always today." Zen Proverb

November 15

"The significance is hiding in the insignificant. Appreciate everything." Eckhart Tolle

November 16

"As long as we have practiced neither concentration nor mindfulness, the ego takes itself for granted and remains its usual normal size, as big as the people around one will allow." Ayya Khema

November 17

"Throughout this life, you can never be certain of living long enough to take another breath." Huang Po

November 18

Be happy in the moment, when possible. Each moment offers us all we need, not more

November 19

"If you live the sacred and despise the ordinary, you are still bobbing in the ocean of delusion." Linji Yixuan

November 20

"We have only now, only this single eternal moment opening and unfolding before us, day and night." Jack Kornfield

November 21

"Perfection of character is this: to live each day as if it were your last, without frenzy, without apathy, without pretence." Marcus Aurelius

November 22

"Guilt, regret, resentment, sadness & all forms of non-forgiveness are caused by too much past & not enough presence." Eckhart Tolle

November 23

It is only when we truly realise that we will begin to live each day.

November 24

"Mindfulness, is the root of Happiness" Joseph Goldstein

November 25

Pure awareness transcends thinking.

November 26

"I'm here to tell you that the path to peace is right there, when you want to get away." Pema Chödrön

November 27

"Every day we are engaged in a miracle which we don't even recognize: a blue sky, white clouds, green leaves, the black, curious eyes of a child - our own two eyes. All is a miracle." Thich Nhat Hanh

November 28

Life is for living- savour every moment.

November 29

"This is the real secret of life — to be completely engaged with what you are doing in the here and now. And instead of calling it work, realize it is play." Alan Watts

November 30

"The real voyage of discovery consists not in seeking out new landscapes but in having new eyes." Marcel Proust

December 1

"Look at the world once again with open eyes. And when you do so, a sense of wonder and quiet contentment begins to reappear in your life." Mark Williams

December 2

"The only way to live is by accepting each minute as an unrepeatable miracle." Tara Brach

December 3

"The moment one gives close attention to anything, even a blade of grass, it becomes a mysterious, awesome, indescribably magnificent world in itself." Henry Miller

December 4

"Today, you can decide to walk in freedom. You can choose to walk differently. You can walk as a free person, enjoying every step." Thich Nhat Hanh

December 5

Pause and pay attention- everything changes when we focus.

December 6

"In today's rush, we all think too much — seek too much — want too much — and forget about the joy of just being." Eckhart Tolle

December 7

"Life is not lost by dying; life is lost minute by minute, day by dragging day, in all the small uncaring ways." Stephen Vincent Benet

December 8

"The art of living… is neither careless drifting on the one hand nor fearful clinging to the past on the other." Alan Watts

December 9

"What would it be like if I could accept life-accept this moment, exactly as it is?" Tara Brach

December 10

Be sensitive to the nuances of every moment.

December 11

"Mindfulness, also called wise attention, helps us see what we're adding to our experiences, not only during meditation sessions but also elsewhere." Sharon Salzberg

December 12

"The fundamental cause of grasping and rejecting, the source of all our pain, relies upon taking things –all our mental projections– as real." Dzigar Kongtrul Rinpoche

December 13

"We use mindfulness to observe the way we cling to pleasant experiences & push away unpleasant ones." Sharon Salzberg

December 14

"It's not about approving or liking, but just being able to allow the world to be the way it is without resenting, hating, or judging it." Buddhist saying

December 15

"My experience is that many things are not as bad as I thought they would be." Mary Doria Russell

December 16

"Suffering usually relates to wanting things to be different than they are." Allan Lokos

December 17

Let us focus on living wholeheartedly, and watch our lives transform.

December 18

"When you are present, you can allow the mind to be as it is without getting entangled in it." Eckhart Tolle

December 19

"We cannot be present and run our story-line at the same time." Pema Chödrön

December 20

Life is short, so try to enjoy every minute.

December 21

"Bíonn adharca fada ar na ba thar lear." Far away cows have large horns (far way hills look green.)

December 22

We withdraw from our experience of the present moment by incessantly telling ourselves stories about what is happening in our life. Pause and observe instead. Life is a magical experience.

December 23

"If you want to conquer the anxiety of life, live in the moment, live in the breath." Amit Ray

December 24

"Stepping out of the busyness, stopping our endless pursuit of getting somewhere else, is perhaps the most beautiful offering we can make to our spirit." Tara Brach

December 25

"The most precious gift we can offer others is our presence. When mindfulness embraces those we love, they will bloom like flowers." Thich Nhat Hanh

December 26

The energy of mindfulness has the elements of friendship, love and kindness in it.

December 27

"Look at other people and ask yourself if you are really seeing them or just your thoughts about them." Jon Kabat-Zinn

December 28

Essentially, meditation allows us to live in ways that are less automatic. This means less time spent worrying and trying to control things we can't control.

December 29

"All beings want to be happy, yet so very few know how. It is out of ignorance that any of us cause suffering, for ourselves or for others". Sharon Salzberg

December 30

"Maireann an chraobh ar an bhfál ach ní mhaireann an lámh do chuir." The branch lives on the hedge but the hand that planted it be dead.

December 31

"Somehow I always seem to forget the most powerful tool I have : myself. My presence." Carla Naumburg

Thank you- Go raibh maith agat

About the Author

Julie has worked for over 30 years in the arena of teaching and training in Ireland, Italy and Australia. She has qualifications in Primary Teaching, Mindfulness, Coaching and Management. She is a Reiki Master and a joint Irish Munster Connecting Consciousness Coordinator with her husband Michael. She is a trained Celtic Priestess and has a profound love for our Celtic land and its Ancient Spiritual traditions.

For more information go to www.solasceremonies.ie

Printed in Great Britain
by Amazon

87668907R00045